Following Ghosts Upriver

poems by
Marc Pietrzykowski

MAIN STREET RAG PUBLISHING COMPANY
CHARLOTTE, NORTH CAROLINA

Copyright © Marc Pietrzykowski 2011

Cover art: "Upside Down Upside Down," by Ashley Pietrzykowski

Author photo by:

Library of Congress Control Number: 2010940257

ISBN: 978-1-59948-265-1

Produced in the United States of America

Main Street Rag
PO Box 690100
Charlotte, NC 28227
www.MainStreetRag.com

ACKNOWLEDGEMENTS

The author wishes to thank the following editors and journals where these poems first appeared:

88: "Stare Decesis."
Barnwood International Poetry Review: "Following Ghosts Upriver, 1"; "Desire Algebraic"; "Good Friday."
deComp: "There's Never a Line."
Labor: Studies in Working-Class History of the Americas: "Economic Development Seminar."
Mastodon Dentist: "The Grinding Wears the Stone Down, Too."
New Zoo Poetry Review : "The Flare."
Skidrow Penthouse: "The Frequency is in the Upper Reaches of the Band."
tinfoildresses: "Following Ghosts Upriver, 2"; "Thank You For Showing Me The Way Home."
Wisconsin Review: "Animal Logic and the Hub."

For Ashley, with gratitude.

CONTENTS

Part 1:

Following The Ghosts Upriver, 1 3
Desire Algebraic 4
Good Friday 6
Animal Logic and the Hub 11
How I Almost Nodded Off Waiting for Her
    to Come Home From Work 12
Executive Privilege 16
Research and Development 18
Mirabilia 19

Part 2

Following The Ghosts Upriver, 2 23
There's Never a Line 26
At the Niagara County Landfill and Recycling Center 28
Economic Development Seminar 29
The Grinding Wears the Stone Down, Too 30
Ice Sculpture 32
In Praise of Winter 33

Part 3

Stare Decesis 37
Carnivalesque 38

The Flare	39
Strategy and Tactics	41
Lunar Spring Thaw	43
House and Door and Window	45
Sonnets are Stupid	46
Thank You For Showing Me The Way Home	47
The Frequency is in the Upper Reaches of the Band	48
Following The Ghosts Upriver, 3	49
Little City Breakdown	51

PART ONE

Even here is a season of rest,
And I to my cabin repair.

—William Cowper, *"The Solitude of Alexander Selkirk"*

FOLLOWING GHOSTS UPRIVER, 1

All these sad, broken towns
strewn with rusted oil drums
and pallets, stacked and rotting,
are my home, every one.
Along the Mohawk, the Niagara,
the oily Genesee,
run the tracks and the trains
and the passengers on their way
somewhere bright, somewhere
with a hint of glamour, somewhere
not like the dead little towns
they have left behind. I was born
under their rooflines, drank
from their sooty wells,
learned that their borders,
stubbled with briar,
were the edges of love; that grace
was a crumpled cardboard box
thrusting a flap skyward
from the sidewalk; and that
the evening fire beckoned to us
from the hearth
because it was dieing.
Watching the streets and the spaces
between them blur by, I know
I have been away too long in places bright
and not so glamorous,
but not so long, a voice humming up
from the engine tells me,
that I have forgotten
how to peel off my shoes
and pull a chair up beside the embers
and start to place my small sticks,
one by one, upon the coals.

DESIRE ALGEBRAIC

First, an aunt, half-asleep after third shift,
drifted across the median
into a school bus. Witness: the crumpled hood
of her just-paid for car, the closed casket,
and the consistency of this closing act
with the rest of her days: no one else
was injured. Weeks later, an old man,
her father, farm-raised and all his life
a prodigious spreader of seed, at last
had enough of his body withering, shrinking
in knobs and folds, so he turned into chaff
and blew away.

After the second funeral, the ghost of Pythagoras
came whispering through the pews: *who,
who will be the third?*
Two is divisible, weak and composed
of lonely symmetries, of ones forced together
so obviously… but three, the triangular,
lends an extra dimension, one that seems
a source of wisdom, and nothing
adds dimension to a coordinate plane
like death—there must be a third,
we cannot make meaning without
proper sacrifice, the latch drawn shut,
the smell of blood, of life underground.

Of course there were no volunteers; instead,
we all took hysterical care while driving,
walking, noticing gratefully
that the Government Building
had no thirteenth floor. Insteard, tonight
we are mathematicians
all, seers waiting for the surge
of wisdom that will come
when the formula is complete,
when three emerges from the collapse of two
and one from naught,
from tziphra, sipos, tsiphron, rota,
circulus, galgal, theca, null, sunya, as-sifr—
from the only number, beneath which
all the others go, the brilliant O, figura nihili.

GOOD FRIDAY

1.
Kneeling in the hayloft, she prays
in winter light. The new calf's bleating
quiets in the stall beneath,
the mother's shuffling hooves, snorts,
all falls a hush. The light prickles
against her eyelids, she prays
into a beam of yellowed heat
that blocks off the path to God:

Gloria in excelsis deo,
et in terra pax hominibus bonae voluntatis
Laudamus te.
Benedicimus te. I cannot see you
O Lord, I cannot hear your voice.
I look in the sun for you
and cannot find you, I search
the skies and fields and the eyes
of my children and cannot
find you. Adoramus te.
Glorificamus te.

Every morning, she breaks a loaf
into six pieces, makes six bundles,
each with perhaps an egg, a piece
of boiled beef, a rind of cheese,
snug beside the bread. Every morning
she sends her husband off to the fields,
theirs' or the landlords'; the older
sons will join him in another year.
And every morning, chores finished,
the children go in a knot up the road
to school, books and bundles astride them.

Only then, once they have gone
over the rise, once her own early chores
are finished, does she climb the hayloft
and pray until her crooked body sways
to the sound of another voice,
and she prays harder, and begs for help,
and no help comes, and she fights
the devil until the corn sheller calls,
until the loom shuttle calls, until
the new calf starts to moan and the chickens
scream from across the yard
at the devil taking flight and his shadow
passing over them.

2.
Her husband worries and is kind,
brings her a book of paper to write in,
a new rosary, fine boots worth more
than they can afford. She fills the boots
with manure and eggshells,
hides the rosary in a coffee can,
opens the book in a rage
and digs the nib into it, the word
is God and God is the word,
black ink squelching the white fire
of the pages.

Lord, I cannot find you,
the Devil has hid you behind the sun,
the world is too bright and I cannot
find you. Gratias agimus tibi propter
magnam gloriam tuam.

Domine Deus, Rex caelestis, Deus Pater omnipotens.
Domine fili unigenite, Jesu Christe.
Save me Lord and I will give you
everything, all that I am all
that I have…

The children look side-eyed
when she dyes all their clothes purple,
underclothes, coats, mittens. The better
to hide in from the Devil's light,
she thinks, watching her husband trudge
off to town to fetch the doctor.

3.
Molly and I found her journal
at a flea market upstate, wedged
between junior league cookbooks.
We sat in the motel and watched
her script grow smaller and smaller,
her prayers reverse light and dark,
her last oath to God and then pages
of black on black, ink scribbled
into dense and moonless thatch.

We read about how the doctor came
and brought her things to drink,
but his potions were of the Devil,
and she poured them on the ground
where they hissed and smoked. We saw
her husband's eyes begin to shine
with the Devil's light, how she crept
up on him with a poker, red from the fire,

how he woke and knocked her down. She
made her final oath, the pages
went black, and she ran out to the barn
to sway there in the quiet dark,
free from the Devil and the blinding light:
Domine Deus, Agnus Dei, Filius patris.
Qui tollis peccata mundi, miserere nobis.
Qui tollis peccata mundi suscipe deprecationem nostram.
Qui sedes ad dexteram patris miserere nobis.
Quoniam tu solus sanctus.
Tu solus Dominus.
Tu solus Altissimus, Jesu Christe.
Cum Sancto Spiritu in gloria Dei Patris. Amen.

Easter two days off, she brushes
the hay from her knees, descends
full of the Lord's light. Her husband is lit
with Devil's flame and yells,
breath reeking of the underworld.
He cannot touch her.
The stairs do not squeak underfoot,
the door swings open before her
though she puts no hand upon it.
She stands in the children's room
and bathes them in the Lord's light.
I will keep my promise.

Tucked in behind the last few pages
a clipped obituary, the youngest boy
who fell from a window Good Friday's
eve and broke his neck. The last legible
page of block letters: MY SON FELL

Following Ghosts Upriver

AND I CULD NOT CATCH HIM.
When Molly closed the book
and sipped from her plastic cup,
I could tell she was staring
at a place out beyond our time together,
past our half-hearted fights and worn-thin
love. I could tell by the way she smiled
as though it was the first time she'd ever seen me.

ANIMAL LOGIC AND THE HUB

The flight to Pittsburgh was oversold
and a voice on the loudspeaker
        begged for volunteers,
for the flexibly scheduled, for *heroes*:
this is how we live. We walk the gangplank
        to a winged metal tube
and are flung to distant cities,
we disembark and wonder at the mess
we've made of our children,
        our parents, our homes,
our gods, our health;
we make do and cringe at the presence
        of other people, we preen
and draw them toward us,
we puff up our chests and laugh
        too loudly, we recoil
when another claims us
as part of some not-so-royal "we."

As it is and always has been,
but further bent into our selves,
as it is and will someday cease to be,
bundles of nerve and blood embroidered
with the sound of pictures, the color
of word, each of us ready, at an instant,
to don the cape and pose on a mound of dead—
to be heroes, and not to fly.

Following Ghosts Upriver

HOW I ALMOST NODDED OFF
(or, I imagine a baby rat in my mouth as I wait for my beloved to come home)

Ah! I hear the screen door slap shut,
    feet clogging down the hallway,
        and then a tap-tap-tapping coming from behind one
            front tooth, my tooth:

these are the sounds my head snaps awake too, the sounds
    of a collapsing rhythm (sleep), sounds (sleep)
        that celebrate their (sleep) demise themselves, old and
                              dying gods
    snuggling up for a last mug of ichor,
sounds lodged in the cracks

of the day-to-day, of our monument thereof,

    the bold, stern faces we war with
        and take charge with and make good time with
        and fuck with, if it's like that,

        build stone faces with, riddled with sparrow-holes,
            with the nests of smaller mites,
                single-celled colonies alive
                      in the soft folds
                          around the eyes—

like the faces alive on my favorite t-shirt, the red one, torn and
                                          threadbare,
    (it mocked the gods of easter island, they
        unlikely to sue for libel)
a stony but slightly animate face, one eyebrow raised
    as though it heard feet coming down the hallway
        (jackbooted feet? No, they're cleverer now,

       feet in soft-soled italian loafers,
       feet clattering in wooden Buddha sandals).

That shirt, my shirt, an expression of perfect paranoia and now stolen,
       stolen by some or another rag-dreamer,
          made into a flag, or—no, now I remember,
              I cast it into the trash in a fit, a fit that demanded:
all outerwear
invested with memory must
            to the discard pile go. (they were creepy, the judge
                and jury and all the rest of the crew that built
                the decree,
            but then I was creepy too, fair bet).

O man, I got that shirt at the state fair, with my moms, no, I
got it at the MOMA Koons exhibit, with Auntie Bedelia, no,
       well, whatever, wherever, I liked that shirt
          but that was a long time ago, I was on a fixed income
              and I moved on, off into the redwoods for a bit
                  then to the city of slaughterhouses.

No more budgets now, I go for splurging, now, wastefulness—
                                          mindful wasting!
       Dragging the earth and all her people down with me.
There are, to wit, weiners presently on the grill,

          weiners roasting within their various names, spitting little seeds
                                                  of hot fat
on the coals; weiners are meant to hiss and sizzle, to speak,
       they say: Robert Vaughn! Robert Vaughn! And what could it
                                                        mean
          but there is Robert Vaughn on the back porch,

Following Ghosts Upriver

on the table, on a kitchen magnet sent
from Gary Myers, attorney-at-law, willing to take my case.

See Robert Vaughn's head leap from the table to my eye!
See how stern his stony face, see how it explodes
into my eye! He was an actor, he played a spy and blah blah blah

and now his stern stony face is a value-added object

that pops! Explodes into the sleepy matrices
    of my recognition! Robert Vaughn,
        on a kitchen magnet, on the small green plastic
            patio table
            that sits on my back porch
            beside an empty Tidy Cats Multi-Cat litter carton
        and the overflowing recycleable bin.
And omigod there really are—mastadonic, furious—footsteps

    coming down the hallway: pull
    the covers to the chin, there are no covers,
    only weiners and a steaming back porch
    and the end of summer, instead: must
                    visualize
           mommy…

        and omigod, turns out it's love making all that racket,
        witless and strong as a dying animal,
        gnaw-your-own-foot-off love,
    my daily habit and all the daily re-enactments
of my daily habit: love-as-it-is, love in the world,
you as the locus of my heart emerging,
    you as the locus of a landscape suddenly gorged with love,

        you as the altar,
              I as the pew, the prayer rug,
                    the bent knee, the folded hand,
                          the eye in perfect focus.
And this is what I fear and celebrate as fear?
These are the sounds turn a face from stone to flesh?

    No more monuments, not stone, not flesh, they make us pigeons,
    they make us slide around in the foam and shit
    trying to draw a bead on glory like it was a life raft
    and not a bag of rocks,
    trying even to harvest the Killer from fields of children,
        to trim the Stoolie from yards of scripture,
            to extract god from the light and the light
        from the ever-popular Waking Moment,
all for a bag of rocks...

    but never mind, where is my shirt? And the tapping behind
my tooth, my tongue hides in the back of my mouth,
        hides from the rat that tries endlessly to dig its way out,
    never succeeds,
whines like a broken fanbelt day in, day out...
        I suppose it's only the nature of rats to try
    and escape,
               and the tap-tap-tapping behind my front tooth
                  that just won't quit.
is only a rat psalm, a way to escape by celebrating
    our inability to escape,

And then the door opens and you smile and my rat sprouts wings—

Following Ghosts Upriver

EXECUTIVE PRIVILEGE

He put his hand in her face
and fumbled with the baffles;
Pretty kitty, pretty kitty,
and an expensive cat at that,
he fumbled with the baffles
until something wrong went "snap"
and kitty slumped.

In line at the business center
pretty kitty in a box
beneath his arm: no surprise
how that turned out, no refund
no return, tech support =
2 pints of plasma/hour.

And he needs his blood to eat,
and his clones all failed
in the summer heat,
his credit stamp a faded smear,
pretty kitty won't get fixed
this year or any year, the way
his luck's been going.

But the office must count
for something, as patriots insist,
and so he broadcasts his plea
on the afternoon feed:
Your President needs your help,
dignity, other heads of state,
Pretty Kitty! Please vote today.

They watch the numbers tick by,
pretty kitty a sack of wires,
Mr. President a sad old man—
sad enough for the referendum
to pass. Tech support, orange suits,
a blur in the oval office:
pretty kitty purrs at last.

RESEARCH AND DEVELOPMENT

Farinelli saw the stars land
and he sang to them his castrati
and the stars turned and ran
back across the filament
and up into their spheres.

*Two is the number of countesses
suicided after I was Adelaide,
one is the number of digits
I gave freely, and would give again,
and naught the number of rude butchers,
maids, farmers, paint-mixers, and dogs
who've ever **run** from my bejeweled voice.*
Thus puzzled, he pressed his head
to a perfumed pillow and slept.

He did not wake when the stars
returned, silent as death;
did not stir as they hovered about him,
thinking at one another;
only dreamed gently as they departed
once again, unable to conceive
a means to strap and mount his voice
beside the pulse cannon at the prow
of their battle cruiser.

MIRABILIA

Mid-morning rain indulges us a pattern
even as it vexes us our parades and al fresco,
hurtling down from the substantial nowhere
we often glimpse when in planes,
wedged in too-narrow seats,
peeking out the too-small windows
at the space between clouds. We have glass-bottomed
boats, and should build jetliners
the same way; Wonder Woman
had a transparent plane,
after all, though explaining
this concept to, say, Roger Bacon
might prove difficult, some rainy mid-morning
in a nook amongst the dreaming spires,
over mead and a table scattered
with lenses and vellum…
better to just buy him a ticket on the Concorde
and a knapsack full of comic books
then meet him at JFK
with a strong cup of coffee
and some Lebanese hash.
He's going to need both, as will you,
before the two of you start working
on nature's veil again, and even if you
are not, and plan instead to spend the evening
lost in the tortured lights of Times Square.

PART TWO

I believe that we are lost here in America, but I believe we shall be found. And this belief, which mounts now to the catharsis of knowledge and conviction, is for me—and I think for all of us—not only our own hope, but America's everlasting, living dream.

—Thomas Wolfe, *"You Can't Go Home Again"*

FOLLOWING GHOSTS UPRIVER, 2

Grinding up through the Cumberland gap
in a rented panel truck
stuffed with boxes of wine and oil,
umbrellas, socks, all the detritus
plucked and condensed from
the Kuiper belt of objects
drawn into orbit by the force of our habits
and our habits' habits;
grinding up from Atlanta
and its nest in the piedmont,
from a New City full of nothing
but a surging tide of options
and derivatives, upon which floats
all the usual trophies desired
by souls who believe money
the fruit of all good. Atlanta is no
sprinting maiden stopping
for golden apples, nor is Hippomenes'
golden youth alive in the sun;
no, it is there, in the stall
at the edge of the crowd,
the one selling souvenir fruit
painted gold, and silver too—
that is where Atalanta lives,
and she carries water and food
in to the merchant, suffers his rapes
and belt, dreams of killing him,
taking over the stall, bronzing his organs
and placing them among the wares…

And so we grind up out of her lap,
over the piedmont, through the gap
into Tennessee, the same verdant, endless

ripple of ridges dusty, pocked soldiers
once stumbled home over,
bred between, built clapboard churches
and radio towers upon,
learned to sell fireworks and horses along...
the truck rocks and strains going up,
rocks and hums going down,
lulls us both but we are together
in America and so each take turns
jarring the other awake. On the plateau
we nod at horses dappling the late
afternoon fields, listen
to preachers shouting about God
and Liberals, about Just Rewards
and Welfare Queens, about the many
Righteous Wars they believe themselves
to be fighting. Night is sudden,
or we missed the last light wink off,
and the trucks take over, headlights
meld into serpents, erupt from
behind crests ahead, blast the interior
of the truck cab and drag boxy shadows
along your sleeping face. Alone

in America, on our way home, Kentucky
and Ohio and Pennsylvania
announcing themselves
from the shoulder, spreading varieties
of highway greenery and cardboard hotels
before us, we have only to stop
and stretch out beside
a gas pump, watch aging motorcyclists

adjust their pants, offer
money to the young cashier, her face
a coiled snake ready to strike,
to understand: we are not alone
in America, or anywhere else;
we are not even ourselves,
but then we get back in the truck
and begin to move again
along the road, to forget
that you and I are fictions,
and then faith creeps in like mold
and the stories start to tell themselves,
and we are: almost there,
hoping we have left behind
Atlanta, the piedmont, all the things
we once drove toward.   The child
cries out in the night not
to see if his mother still exists
but to remind himself that he does;
so it is with the highways
of America, each car a cozy bed
sliding over monsters too slow
to catch us, every mile
another cry meant to dispel
the blind and murderous night.

THERE'S NEVER A LINE

In a desperate little restaurant
filled with small-town lawyers
and legislators, fat and rosy,
where the table sags and we sag
with it, where the waitress tries
to keep from crying, we
smile and pile our dishes for her,
we brush crumbs from the table
and rub our bellies happily,
but not too happily, though the meal
was made from blood and song.

Eyes and the top of a head appear
in the window of the swinging door,
peep you, and disappear; you tell me
we're being watched, and I say yes,
I know, we are the guts of a lamb,
the paths of doves flung into the sky,
the cracks splintering an oracle bone.
The eyes, the waitress, the fearful
men in shopworn suits, all are trying
to read us: are they
wealthy investors? Hired killers?
Merely lost? And there is no way
for us to reply: no, we live here now,
we are like you, hidden chef,
sad-eyed server, small-time
power-monger.

There is no way because
we are not like them yet,
we have too many things to forget,
too many new steps to learn

before we find ourselves
peeking out at the new faces, trying
to draw strength and some future tense
from the curve of an unfamiliar neck,
the set of the shoulders, from the way
they wipe their mouths, then recede
back into the loam of somewhere else.

AT THE NIAGARA COUNTY LANDFILL AND RECYCLING CENTER
(or, The Believer Among Us)

Seraphim, cherubim, from cut earth they rise,
from pipes bent like hooks, emerging, they rise,
ophanim glaze upwards, the muddy sky
shimmers, the air bent with angels
who sing as they rise.

                                          At his throne
Stavros sits, from his throne calls down judgment
on the truck that now idles, now straddles the scale.
The weights are recorded, the angels are witness,
malakhim, hashmallim, they watch from above,
over mud the wheels go, elohim, they roll,
and Stavros is left to watch the air glow.

With black fire he numbers, on white fire
records them, while archangels whisper
the trisagion: *Agios o Theos, agios ischyros,
agios athanatos, eleison imas.*
From the throats of the angels,
as the grumbling trucks pass,
the song quakes through Stavros
like garbage to gas.

Marc Pietrzykowski

ECONOMIC DEVELOPMENT SEMINAR

The blast furnace quakes to life, the girders
        spidered up around it
shudder in sympathy, then the rivets start
        to keen… it's been dead thirty months,
the tower and conveyor, the furnace dome,
        the skimmer; thirty months
since slag oozed out, thirty months since any pig iron
        squealed free from a chunk of hematite.

Fall has daubed the world from the edges inward
        with mud and honey and ash
and ghosts swing from the porches and wait
        for the mendicants to come,
begging sweets. A hole in the chain link fence
        bordering veteran's park
grants egress to teens and vagrants,
        spills them out onto the railroad tracks
and the rusted boxcars strewn
        like pieces of type on a printer's floor.

Most nights, when they meet
        on the path—the teens gangling free
from their falling houses
        and the rooted hobos who dig loaves
from dumpsters—they glance
        side-eyed across time at each other, giggle,
mutter, move on, but tonight, with the smell
        of burning coke and limestone
tinting the air, the young ones offer
        skittish hellos, the old men grimace
and hand them bottles of wine,
        and they stand together for a moment
watching the flames lick at the stars.

THE GRINDING WEARS THE STONE DOWN, TOO

These were the days of the week: 6 am: rise, evacuate, preen,
mumble at the pigeons on the ledge.
Morning light hissing up from the underworld
as I made toast. Butter for you, jelly for me,
7 am: kiss-and-part, ache, endure,
then home again and, perhaps, the weight of you.

          And thus I became a cretin,
fat
and grateful
for every little jelly stain
and buttery lip. Home by 6 most days of the week,
weekends a fog of crumpled sheets
and tree-lined strolls; these were the scenes that dug
a hole in my skull, trepanned me
and let all the wrong of this world leak out.
Specific details are nothing, they make you a fool,
a town idiot fumbling with beads and string—
they will make you a believer,
          and that should be warning enough.

Use my example, tack my photo
to kindergarten walls: this is what happens when you believe
that details add up to something more
than another detail, this is what happens
when 5 pm comes, when the train shudders into the station,
your hands stained, your ears full of chatter, your dank stairs,
your oven lit, your glass of vodka, the stupid way you sit
and wait. Wait to hear a key
squeak the lock. To feel a hand
upon your neck. For all details

to fade into mush, for the truck
to come and haul away her clothes,
for the lake to swallow her ashes
and turn them into fish. This is what belief
gets you, children: half a man,
surrounded by details,
waiting to be rid of them and all that they insinuate.

ICE SCULPTURE

The bus chugs on between mounds of snow.
She watches it go, then tugs open her scarf
to let the cold start to kiss her throat;
at home, she'll prop the window up and let
the clean night air come stroke her 'till she floats
away, to become the beat of her heart
slowed, her body at rest, free from knowledge.

The dogs who live next door whine and wake her;
a door opens, they tumble down the stairs
and bark and bounce and shit. She grits her teeth,
then to herself recites her morning prayer:
"I swear upon my mother's grave, I'll kill
those dogs one day." She hears them tumble back
upstairs, hears the owner coo, smells an egg
start to fry, and tries to stay perfectly still.

IN PRAISE OF WINTER

A circle of leaves the color
      of just-ripe lemons
glows in the the yard, a sky as gray
      and pocked as concrete
seethes above them; no, the world
is not upside down: it's early November
      in Western New York, go,
stuff the chinks with paper, go,
split your logs and clean the radiators.

Murder will wait 'till March, or April; now
      is the time of bells
waiting to be struck. Incurious sapling
teens rush and twitter along the sidewalk
      homeward to their video clusters,
incurious pulpy adults appear
      and blow lemony leaves
down and over the curb; everyone
cannot stand still and everyone
walks slightly hunched, cowering, dogs
      sensing a raised hand.
The bell will soon sound, the earth
      will vanish
and whiten and grow slick.
I keep my heathen prayers to myself:
I can scarcely wait to taste the first flakes,
to feel the first uncontrollable shudder,
the wind that turns my bones to glass.

Squirrels fat as bankers stop to watch
      my small dance, my snow
prayer: head cocked, peering at the sky,

a coarse wind shears up over the escarpment
and blows the folds of my coat open.
        I pull it back against my waist
and laugh. Five months of dark, cold,
        and sleet, a tunnel stretching
from autumnal wealth to the first
nude shoots of spring. There is a snarl
        of wires in my brain
and it blinks out a code, the story
written on the walls of the dome
it grew beneath: ice, thaw, burn, harvest,
        then prepare for ice again.

I keep my heathen prayers to myself,
white-lipped, quivering, waiting for the song
of snow, the deathless wind
that mocks the embers
even as it teases them back to flame.

PART THREE

Here the children snozzle at milk bottles, children who have never seen a cow.
Here the stranger wonders how so many people remember where they keep home fires.

—Carl Sandburg, *"Home Fires"*

STARE DECESIS

Doves in fist, campfire visible from the valley,
we settled down among the lemon trees.
We sat and bled the doves beside the fire and ate.

Every third Saturday the pastor came and slept,
and three times a year we visited him,
and once a year we did nothing all day long.

We tried to love one another because we snap like dolls,
and when we went up into the mountains, looking
for doves, we sang about the trees burning down.

Once upon a time I heard a song of riches,
endless doves perched on cedar limbs.
but then again, once upon a time, I was a child.

CARNIVALESQUE

In every town lives the woman who never bathes
and talks into a dead cell phone she pulled from a dumpster,
and in every town lives the man whose face
sprouts new sores daily, whose nose holds broken glasses
                        five times too large
suspended over stolen false teeth
                        three times too small.
Every town has them, but ours are in charge.

Hence, the street lights burn a pale green,
hence the bell tower is slanted
and the bell stuffed with dead gulls.
The alleyways and rooflines
burn words of fire into the skull,
and the keys to the city are given to anyone who asks,
                        though the keyhole has great rusty fangs.

The voice in the dead cell phone tells her to walk
and we have a parade; his false teeth fall
into the canal and we hold our annual fishing derby.
You probably don't understand,
                        if you're not from around here,
why we like things the way they are,
and the only way really to explain it
is to ask what other places are like
and then shake our heads, ashamed
at such atrocities, such savagery,
astounded at how a soul must suffer
when trapped in tidy lands, ruled by wise old kings.

Marc Pietrzykowski

THE FLARE

When the bird came down the chimney
And shrieked over the dinner table
Into the den, father chased after
With a blanket, and we trailed behind
Like kites. Trapped under a wool
Coverlet printed with green trout,
The bird beat its wings, leapt
And thrashed, made a muffled noise
Like a heart gone mad, even as father
scooped and gathered the ends
of the blanket in his hands.

Out in the snow, flung from
The blanket, the bird lay still and twitched
One wing. *Is it broken?* As we fell
To whispering, no one saw
It fly away, but all at once the little hole
In the snow was empty save for
A few brown feathers. Walking

From the barn, thirty-five years later,
I saw a hole with exactly the same
Shape and color and feathery
Texture, but forming out
On the horizon, immense,
Hovering, across a snowy field of stubble.
All at once I felt something beat
Its wings inside my chest, felt it leap
And thrash; before I could
Spill it out onto the snow, something else
Awoke, beneath my feet and the earth
And beneath space and it rose up

To the flutter in my chest
and consumed it in a burst of light.

The flare has stayed in my skull
Like the ghost of a flash bulb
For months, dim and lurking
In a corner while I cut hay or watch
The new foal wobble about,
But it brightens as if to blind me
When I forget, and start to think
About mexicans taking all the jobs
Or how stupid my children are
Or how glad I am the wife died
When she did. It must be cells
Gone crazy in my brain, tumors
On top of tumors. Time is short.
Yesterday I stood, staring

At my car keys in a parking lot
Like the story of the universe
Was written in their grooves,
The way they suck light in,
Spit it back out again, the shadow
And filigree and brassy glare
Played their music on my eyes
Until I cried for the thirteenth time
That day, at nine o-clock in the morning.

STRATEGY AND TACTICS

The cat's head swelled and grew transparent
'till it filled the room, the sound of breathing
and little pips of synapse floating over my bed.
I could not raise an arm to wipe it away,
to thrash and tear the wispy skull;
when she began to purr, black water came
and swallowed me.
                       When I woke,
she was gone, off cleaning herself
or reporting to central cat command the results
of the latest experiment, how quickly
the drugs secreted in my kielbasa
had taken effect.
            I am a willing subject, of course,
since I love her so and the way she shapes
my life. I scoop her shit from a box
and make it clean for her, I rub her
until she swipes at me and lays long red
tracks on my arm. Many's the worse arrow
I've suffered in exchange for love
and companionship; if I must be a cog
in the ongoing feline occupation, so be it.

Other forces are at play, as well; why not
throw my lot in with the kitties?
When the television clicks on in the dark
and hard, fractal faces begin to spiral
in and out of themselves, laughing and calling
my dead soul to puppet life, I bear them
but offer no love, I swear to do
                       what they ask
and I lie, go on about the business of living,

such as it is. I would throw my lot
in with the kitties and must, soon,
because I cannot lie forever, they will know,
they are probably reading this now,
over my shoulder, planning the height
of the judge's chair, rising the blood fever
of the jury, polishing the manacles
in anticipation of the next moonless night.

LUNAR SPRING THAW

Across the street a little girl screams
the way only children can: a scream
of delight, but still, every grown-up
in every yard turns their head to check.

She is taunting gravity with a puddle,
splashing banana-yellow boots down
into the muddy meltwater, drops
arcing out into space or bending back
to speckle the hem of her pink coat
and her improbably white leggings,
even up to the gleaming red coil
of her face.

She screams again when her mother
backhands her cheek, doubles its color,
and then once more as she is yanked
by the arm up to the house. More heads turn,
tsk, tsk, turn away. Above them, the moon
just now clearing the roofline is pocked
and scarred wherever bits of dust and rock
and ice have struck her, because the moon
has no atmosphere, all her scars come
in silence. Here on earth, scars
come silent and deafening and all
frequencies between, and so
we who are mostly water
must learn to build, layer by layer,
our own atmospheres, stripes of
troposphere, stratosphere, mesosphere,
sheathing to deflect
the smallest bolides and break

Following Ghosts Upriver

larger ones into fragments that flame
the night sky, so we might
make wishes at them.

But some among us never learn the trick
and instead remain as moons, noiseless
and present, craters and pocks aglow
for all to see, waxing and waning,
tugging the oceans of human love
to and fro. This night, the moon seems
to take up the whole of the sky, lighting
the street bone-blue; in such light
the girl's mother comes out to the street
again, screaming herself now, into a cell phone.
In the upstairs window a small face, freshly
scrubbed, ashen, watching her mother's body
bend and twitch and dream of velocity.

HOUSE AND DOOR AND WINDOW

Becalmed in the moment after a fight
my wife and I retreat to our respective
corners and listen to the washing machine
as it creaks and thuds, its belt worn,
its drum running crooked; it creaks
and thuds and then hits a new cycle,
one that makes a noise like the slow,
ponderous flapping wings of a bird
the size of a jetliner, the very one
now interposing itself between my eyes
and the squared sunlight, soaking it up
until I can no longer see her, or
myself.
        So I fumble about, blind and waving
my hands in little half-circles until they hit
something solid, something wooden
and cold, and I turn it over with my fingers
and then walk on, still holding the thing,
praying silently that I have not left
the cellar door open.

SONNETS ARE STUPID

Everyone looks stupid when they run,
even the graceful and swift: the cheetah
looks stupid, a clump of meat and muscle
and nail and tooth, stupidly angling

toward an ibix, too stupid to starve.
And everyone looks stupid while they fuck,
though not many of us care, or we care
because we are taking stupid aim at

babymaking, a whole stupid family tree:
*"Certain stupid creatures, walking upright,
can shape the steam rising from their heads
into phonetic clusters: air? stone? fire?
gravity? the red moon? Stupid titles
given to the galaxies astride them."*

THANK YOU FOR SHOWING ME THE WAY HOME
—for Ashley

There's this man, and he's telling us about
another man whose memory was blasted
apart, every six seconds he restarts, the world
is new and it's 1956, because it started then,
his endless loop.

The story sets me sprawling along
fevered byways, neuronal speculative
storms, impossible things, like:

        how could it ever
come to pass
that I no longer recognize
your face, in summer slanted light,
whispering to me, smiling softly?
My own brain is already damaged enough
from love that I cannot even think it,
I may as well fail to recognize my own
body surrounding me.

        And so, because it may, in fact,
come to pass that my brain is blasted
and left in less exotic shreds, I've come
        to offer you
these words—not much, I know,
but that's what I have to give, and before you
        were my life I had
not even such a little thing
as a poem
of love.

THE FREQUENCY IS IN THE UPPER REACHES OF THE BAND

That is, the frequency with which I take water up to the fire god,
the god that rides me when I am on fire
and alone. Ha, a brave way to put it, "fire god,"
a brave name he's given him, brave for the patron
of self-love. The frequency with which
I take water to him is alarming to both of us,
but both profit: I am ridden and made
to pull at the bit, he gets steam. To be ridden
breaks the loneliness up into bytes and pixels,
and I have no idea what he does with the steam.
A fair trade. Our chins wiggle, we slink away afterward
like opposing lawyers who've just shared a foul joke
about the afternoon judge.

Love is hemorrhaging out of where the scab used to be,
I can feel the wet running slowly along my skin,
pushing down small hairs like lava over pine
and I like it, I am a factory of love and you,
my precious, provide me planks and ores and electricity
enough for a nation meant to infect all the globe
with color. And yet you are away, our suppliers are turning
their work over to shadowy sub-contractors: world
domination will have to wait, and so
the frequency with which I slip a nail
under the scab and pry it up is alarming, I like it.
I like it and carry water up the little knoll and drown
the little god over and over again; only such discipline
assures that I do not drown you,
when you return, in love, in blood, in fire, in steam, in all of it.

Marc Pietrzykowski

FOLLOWING GHOSTS UPRIVER, PART 3

A fat belly in your 40's makes rise
the risk of dementia, of statistics
proving the knoll we cannot see around
is really there, or at least some angle
of descent, some topographical tic,
is quantifiable, it cannot be
that the science we make things alive with
is so frail, we must believe it, we must,

but not to the point of action, of course,
though my fat belly is nearly 40,
and I did climb the stairs repeatedly
today, if only to move dull green boxes
overfilled with Christmas sparkles and bulbs
up to the third floor. Wasn't belly-fear
made me climb, although belly-fear's the source
of not a few inglorious moments
in my life, and I'm not sure dementia
didn't reach me some time ago. Oh well,

another one for the newspaper pile
that teeters on the dog food bin, threatens
to turn our kitchen into Manila;
maybe some day we'll live on it, squatting
in the refuse while columnists
argue the use-value of our labor.
Or else our fat bellies will drive us mad,
mad and trapped in swells of snow shoulder-high,
not even some rich man's trash heap to feed on.

That's how things are up near the cataract,
up near where the Niagara trips over rock
and out further too, where wrinkled fields

Following Ghosts Upriver

hang between lake and river, the escarpment
run through the middle like a washing line.

It is hard here, but not dire; our dump
remains buried, farms abound and flourish;
we have, in other words, an excellent
view of America's descent into
sludge and grime. Think of it as a kind of

water-park ride, where at the end you must
suffocate in bad debt and discarded
tires. Not so bad, much better than most,
livable enough to write poems, sure. Example:
walking home after too much whiskey
I met a boy with a mouth full of spit
and a brain muddled by constant want;
I gave him my change and told him not to join
the army; war is mean and a bad virus to catch
but anyway, I just knew they'd never have him,
I hoped to save him one more indignity
piling on. Weeks later I saw his picture

in the local paper, arrested for molesting
an 11-year old girl. Maybe the army was not
such a bad idea after all. This is where we live,
America falling over rocks, in slow motion,
and no amount of threats to my 40-year old belly
is going to stop me from pouring a few more
glasses into it, not while I've reason enough
and time and the moon overhead and love
everywhere, not while such evidence
remains hidden to goddamn nearly everyone.

LITTLE CITY BREAKDOWN

Animals taught us to be in the world,
and we abused the lesson

not in our murdering, but in killing
without sacrifice. For example: the city council meeting:
        monkey-brained bureaucrats

clawing each other to death
on a low stage, shooting slides

writ with rules of jurisprudence
onto a white canvas screen,—

a hundred sets of teeth grinding,
        the sound of skinks snapped in two by the pump-shed hinge:—

mutation or virus, whatever it was
made us so wordy and dense,
made us lose track of those we've killed,

may be only the echo of myself lashing myself together

from scraps of all the stories I've heard.
All of them. But because I am an echo
I might be the real thing, and the virus or mutation
makes me say fuck it anyway, who cares when
a pot of basil growing please me and the spot on your
        neck where the hairs stand up please me and the nasty look I
get from everyone sometimes please me   and the sound of
goats please me and all
        the baseball cards I stole and then lost please me
        and offering the whole archipelago to the enemy please me and
god in his monkey-day

tweeds please me and we took the day together to walk in the
autumn light and hold one another, and that, that is all there is…

and once it has pleased me, and then,
and then all the cars shrunk into the void
and all the car stereos shrunk into the void
and all the fire hydrants shrunk into the void
and all the ice cream shrunk into the void
and all the birch trees shrunk into the void
and all the flavored lozenges
and all the magma that all of it sat on shrunk into the void
and all the world thus shrunk into the void
and I was pleased, and you were pleased,
and you are the one I remember
and lie with
and live with and then I can hear the

—-terror systems alert—-

insects, clouds of them,
just outside the window. The cat's paw
beneath the door, pink and grasping,
the pulpy hot tang of fresh chlorine
from the neighbor's pool.

An infinity of compassion spurts across the universe
like ink on silk, sliding, settling, soaking in;
she presses to me, the winged ants
have moved on to the blackberry bushes clotting the fence,
the cat cleans herself at the end of the bed.

The stone that holds the story of walls in its heart,
the dirt that surrenders air, the water pleasing itself in courtyards

and hovels,
that which keeps us alone in grief, alone in the bosom of dark waters,
the sun shining like an axe, day or night,
animals teaching us to be in the world,
viruses teaching us to love—

she presses to me with the entirety of space.